Contents

I0429918

Introduction   1

Section 1: Overview and Objectives   3

Section 2: Plenary Speakers   6

Section 3: Work Group Breakout Sessions   20

Section 4: Conclusions and Recommendations   23

ANNEX A: Selected Question and Answers Sessions 27

ANNEX B: Workshop Attendees   36

"IN THE DARK"

Military Planning for a Catastrophic Critical Infrastructure Event Workshop

The damage level could be sufficient to be catastrophic to the Nation, and our current vulnerability invites attack.
—EMP Commission Report, 2004

Critical national security and homeland defense missions are at an unacceptably high risk of extended outage from failure of the electric grid.
—Defense Science Board, Feb 2008

The earth is situated in a strategic location just 93 million miles from its sun. Since its creation it has survived the cataclysms of temperature extremes, meteor bombardments, and solar storm events. It has survived these events so well that life, including humans, has flourished and prospered in increasing numbers and progressively higher standards of living. For all but the last 150 years, the infrastructure constructed for better human living standards has been relatively unaffected by localized geological disasters or the broader effects of solar storms. But the harnessing of electrical power, begun in the mid-nineteenth century and its distribution via an interconnected grid to which 86% of the U.S. population is now connected, has created the potential for a near certain catastrophe of unprecedented proportion if it fails. The loss of electrical power and communications infrastructure for days, weeks, and more than a year are threat scenarios which could disintegrate the social, agricultural, and governmental fabric which makes a modern society possible today.

The preservation of the electric grid is central to the defense of the United States. To assess the state of preparedness of the United States in the event of the loss of critical infrastructure, especially of electrical and communications infrastructure, the Center of Strategic Leadership at the U.S. Army War College conducted a three day workshop which assembled a body of subject matter experts, civic leaders, and electric industry providers to create awareness, discuss threat postures, and recommend actions to better prepare for the possibility of a critical infrastructure failure or collapse of the electrical grid and associated electronic devices due to either a solar storm, electromagnetic pulse (EMP), or a cyber attack.

As described by specific workshop presenters, solar storms come in 11-year intensity cycles. During these cycles, the sun produces solar flares which eject massive bursts of plasma sometimes in the direction of earth. The plasma emits electrical radiation at all wavelengths, affects the geomagnetic field of the earth, and can induce a current in all electricity conducting wires and components such as radios, computers, and automobile electronics as well as the components of the electric grid itself. The radiation can be of such intensity that these materials would be destroyed in seconds. The most serious threat to the electric grid would be the destruction of power transformers which would take months or years to restore on a national scale. Similarly, not only can this destruction be produced by naturally occurring solar storms, but the same damaging effect can be replicated by a nuclear weapon and other man-made interference devices through malicious intent. A well-placed deliberate nuclear attack at high altitude by a hostile party can produce radiation emissions which can destroy a nation's critical infrastructure. Although there is nothing that can reduce the likelihood of solar flare activity, defense against a nuclear attack is part of national defense. And given that neither solar nor nuclear EMP events can be escaped with certainty, the aftermath of the loss of the effected critical infrastructure must be planned and prepared for. Lastly, high-end cyberspace attacks, such as shutting down various supervisory control and data acquisition (SCADA) systems controlling power generation and distribution throughout the nation, offer a significant threat to critical infrastructure loss that must be defended against. Some cyber threats were addressed in this workshop. A separate Cyberspace Operations Workshop was conducted at the U.S. Army War College, June 15-17, 2010, and that report can be found under a separate cover.

This workshop addressed the preparation, response, and recovery from a catastrophic event. An event may be considered catastrophic when the number of people affected is greater than that normally covered by a typical federal response area and the time to recover was well beyond that of a localized disaster. Also, catastrophic events involve almost complete disruption of communications and other critical infrastructure (such as the electrical power grid). A spectrum chart (Figure 1) helps to illustrate the factors and scope of emergency events that may require the response of organizations at the local, state, and federal levels. The vertical axis of the diagram represents the number of people affected and the horizontal axis represents the time to recover from a given event. Some examples are weather events (such as floods and hurricanes); geological events (such as earthquakes or tsunamis); and biological events (such as an influenza outbreak).

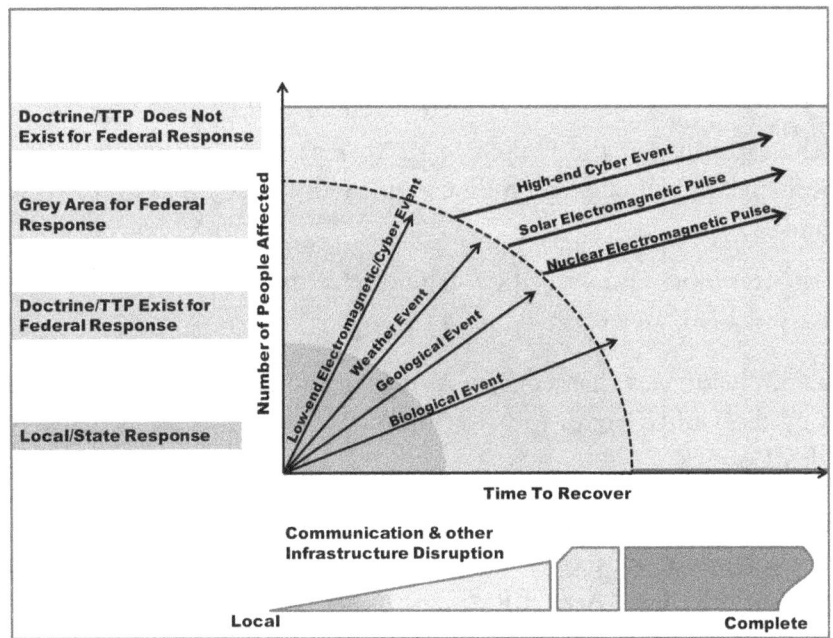

Figure 1: A Spectrum of Catastrophic Events

This report contains four main sections and two annexes. Section 1, Workshop Overview and Objectives; Section 2, Plenary Session Presentation Discussions; Section 3, Break-out Session Findings; and Section 4, Workshop Conclusions and Recommendations. Annex A contains selected questions and answers from the plenary session, and Annex B a list of workshop attendees.

SECTION 1: Overview and Objectives

Congress established an EMP Commission in 2001 and reestablished the commission in 2006 to look at EMP threats and vulnerabilities and what and how the United States would do to recover from an EMP event. The duties of study by the EMP Commission included assessing the following (found at http://www.empcommission.org/):

1. The nature and magnitude of potential high-altitude EMP threats to the United States from all potentially hostile states or non-state actors that have or could acquire nuclear weapons and ballistic missiles enabling them to perform a high-altitude EMP attack against the United States within the next 15 years;

2. The vulnerability of United States military and especially civilian systems to an EMP attack, giving special attention to vulnerability of the civilian infrastructure as a matter of emergency preparedness;

3. The capability of the United States to repair and recover from damage inflicted on United States military and civilian systems by an EMP attack; and

4. The feasibility and cost of hardening select military and civilian systems against EMP attack.

The Commission was charged with identifying any steps it believes should be taken by the United States to better protect its military and civilian systems from EMP attack.

The EMP Commission is no longer active, but its conclusions are every bit as relevant and important today. The Grid Reliability and Infrastructure Defense (GRID) Act (the Grid Act, H.R. 5026) passed the House of Representatives on Jun 9, 2010, but has not yet been acted on in the Senate. However, failure to enact H.R. 5026 into law should not cause delay in educating the general public as to the consequences of the loss of critical infrastructure, nor taking on the challenge of organization, planning, and provisioning for such a calamity.

A 2009 Defense Science Board report, "Unconventional Operations Concepts and the Homeland," looked specifically at the sorts of threats to the Homeland pointed out by the EMP Commission and what the Department of Defense (DOD) should be doing to prepare for them. An examination of issues raised in the Defense Science Board report was the genesis of this workshop. This three-day event served to bring together representative subject matter experts from the EMP commission, lawmakers and elected officials at the state and local level, executives from the power industry, first responders from fire and police departments, and military planners from the Army and Joint commands, and concerned industry leaders who see the need for action in this matter of paramount importance without the expectation of financial gain.

Section 2 of this report will highlight the talking points from each of the plenary session speakers. Each speaker synopsis is intended to be a faithful representation of the session, although certain details, audience remarks, and visual media are necessarily omitted. Some speakers opened their presentation to a question and answer period, and where applicable, that discussion can be found in Annex A.

The objective of the workshop was to gain momentum for the cause of civic action, leadership initiative, and resource investment to ensure that the population of the United States can be prepared as best as possible in the event of the loss of critical infrastructure. The participation of the attendees was broad enough in scope such that each could return to their respective constituencies and plant seeds for this campaign and inject urgency within their domains.

Welcoming remarks to the attendees of the workshop were first made by Mr. Bill Waddell, Director of the Cyber Space Operations Group, Science and Technology Division, Center for Strategic Leadership. Mr. Waddell moderated the overall workshop as well as break-out Group B. The Deputy Commandant of the U.S. Army War College, Colonel Bobby Towery, expressed that the conduct of the workshop was vitally important to our nation since our critical infrastructure is both our lifeline and our Achilles heel. He emphasized that military installations require partnerships with civilian agencies and authorities and that agreements are needed to formalize this mutual involvement. He reminded the audience that September is catastrophic preparedness month and that not enough has been done to plan for the consequence of an infrastructure failure event.

Lastly, Colonel Jim Markley Director of Science and Technology, Center for Strategic Leadership, welcomed everyone on behalf of Professor Doug Campbell, the Director of Center for Strategic Leadership. Colonel Markley expressed his appreciation for the large participation of local, state, national and private organizations at this workshop. As an example of the importance of this gathering, Colonel Markley pointed to recent information about a worm called Stuxnet that was designed to attack critical infrastructures. A worm like Stuxnet was once only theoretical; now it is a reality and poses a potential threat to domestic critical infrastructure. He went on to state that most everyone should have heard of the National Response Framework and its annexes, which detail DODs leading and supporting roles in response to national emergencies. Colonel Markley also pointed to the 2009 Defense Science Board report, which calls for an examination of the DOD in a leadership role in response and consequence management efforts when the scope of an attack on the homeland is sever and widespread. This report is essentially a wake-up call for the DOD which indicates that current plans are insufficient. Colonel Markley asked rhetorically "What are local and state expectations of federal government and the military; where do I need to get in line and what can I expect?" The expectation is that the DOD will fill in all gaps and take care of what others cannot, but this expectation needs to be examined and tempered with the DOD's traditional defense missions. We will be looking at requirements for the DOD during this workshop.

SECTION 2: Plenary Speakers

Mr. Thomas Pappas, *U.S. Army Training and Doctrine Command G-2 – Director, Analysis and Production/Threat.* Mr. Pappas set the stage for the workshop from the vantage point of the U.S. Army Training and Doctrine Command's threat analysis by reviewing six mega trends, five vulnerabilities, and seven threats that face U.S. security interests.

Among the trends, vector oriented operations was the first presented and pertains to organizations with no real leader, but rather people *en masse* that are driven by an ideology and enabled by technology such as the internet. Next, there is an increase in competition for resources, noting that there are now more treaties for water than any other treaties in the world. Globalization is a trend which binds world economies together and awakens the "have nots" with the knowledge that others have more which produces discord and unrest. The proliferation of weapons of mass destruction continues to increase to where "basement" bio and chemical labs are ubiquitous and more countries are building nuclear reactors. Fifth on Mr. Pappas' trend list is the nexus of criminals who are being financed for weaponry to do us harm. Lastly, enemies of the United States are taking technologies of developed nations and ingeniously adapting them for nefarious purposes, such as improvised explosive devices.

Mr. Pappas then outlined five significant vulnerabilities. The United States has an exposed technology base that potential enemies can readily adapt, and do so cheaply. The U.S. infrastructure (104 nuclear reactors, mines, roads, bridges, airports) is exposed and there are insufficient funds to protect all of them. Cultural fault lines are being drawn, and rather than being a melting pot nation, the United States is composed of religious and political groups, plus hundreds of hate groups. The expanding information enterprise can be a global network platform which can be used against our nation by anonymous enemies gaining asymmetric advantage. Retrenchment of the continental U.S. military and multiple deployments makes the United States vulnerable to attack.

Mr. Pappas presented seven specific threats to the United States. First was the threat of extremists who would not hesitate to take down the electric grid and take credit for it. Next among threats was cyber warfare, citing the recent

Stuxnet virus and the hacking of Estonian internet services. Leap-ahead technologies, and the immense amount of information on the internet, enable the threat of EMP weapon devices. International crime was fourth on the threat list and involves complex web of money and money laundering, cartels, law enforcement resources, and death rates which exceed losses in Iraq and Afghanistan. Foreign intelligence services continue to proliferate, and both enemy and friendly units collect data and technology which compromise U.S. security and competitiveness. The sixth threat comes from "trusted insiders" who pass codes and documents to other governments. Lastly, the emerging challenge to U.S. space supremacy will continue. Already, seventy nations have space agencies and several have nuclear capability. (See Q&A at Annex A)

Mr. John Kappenman, *Storm Analysis Consultants*. Mr. Kappenman gave a comprehensive presentation on the origin and impact of severe solar flares, nuclear EMP, and intentional electromagnetic interference (IEMI) on the electric grid infrastructure. Solar activity which produces solar flares and geomagnetic storms can interfere with and impact earth technology and infrastructures. EMP can be caused by the detonation of a nuclear device at high attitude (above 30 km) by a hostile nation or rogue group and could also result from successful interception of nuclear missiles at high altitudes. Such a device does not require sophistication. Non-nuclear IEMI has a limited area of impact but can be used in coordinated attack with a risk scenario comparable to cyber attack. Both geomagnetic storms and the E3 (slow transient) portion of EMP attacks can have the same detrimental effect on large high voltage transformers on the power network, while the E1 (fast transient) portion of EMP and IEMI can both have similar impacts to the electronic equipment and supervisory control and data acquisition (SCADA) systems.

Geomagnetic storms are disturbances in the earth's normal geomagnetic field caused by solar activity. Rapidly changing geomagnetic fields over large regions will induce geomagnetic-induced currents to flow in the continental interconnected electric power grids. Such current flows in transformers will produce half-cycle saturation which can cause power grid blackouts and damage. Two probable areas of greatest impact are the nation's Northwest and the area from the Midwest to the East coast (eastern third of the U.S.) where results can be catastrophic. Permanent damage to the grid can result and take years to repair or replace. If several regions are affected simultaneously, the difficulty of restoring the electric grid is greatly increased. There are several examples which give an indication of the potential impact of geomagnetic storms on the failure of the electric grid. One such example was the geomagnetic super-storm over the North American grid, 13-14 March 1989. Magnetic disturbances were felt all along the U.S.–Canadian border, and much of eastern Canada (Quebec) blacked out in 92 seconds. Manitoba and Minnesota came almost to this point as the storm moved throughout the United States, and there were significant operating anomalies all across the northern third of the country. Latent effects of the geomagnetic storm are suspected of causing about a dozen nuclear power transformer incidents within 25 months after the March 1989 event. Large flares near the center of the sun may set up conditions to start a geomagnetic storm on earth. A flare and associated coronal mass ejection (CME), when pointed toward the earth, can set up conditions for geomagnetic storms. Today, power grids should expect storms four to ten times more intense than the 1989 storm. Historically these occur about every 50 to 100 years, (the last great storm was May 1921).

Significantly, the impact of any damage from a geomagnetic (or other EMP) event increases as our infrastructure increases. The most likely scenario is a CME series in rapid succession, injecting energy into the earth's geomagnetic field. It takes hours for the energy to dissipate, so each CME passage increases the momentum, storing energy from the storms. Large geomagnetic induced currents (GICs) are possible at low latitudes and for a significantly long duration. Long duration GICs can destroy large high voltage transformers as happened in October-November 2003 in Africa when five major stations including 15 large transformers were severely damaged. This storm was about the same intensity as the 1989 storm but longer in duration.

There is new awareness about the extremes of severe geomagnetic storms. Past design practices for electric grids have unknowingly and greatly escalated the risks and potential impacts of such storms. The government forecasters use a measure called a K-index to quantify disturbances in the horizontal component of earth's magnetic field. The K-index does not accurately communicate the real risks to the electric power industry, leaving a false sense of security. Of equal and maybe more immediate threat is that of EMP. The impact of EMP was first noted during nuclear testing in the Pacific Ocean (the STARFISH PRIME event on 9 July 1962) which caused electric grid and telecommunications interference in Hawaii. Today we understand that a high altitude nuclear EMP burst over Columbus, Ohio would expose about 75% of the entire country's electric power substations to damage. Non-nuclear intentional electromagnetic interference (IEMI) weapons can be highly portable and concealable, self-contained in a briefcase (antenna, battery and energy source), and can be designed very easily. A trailer can carry a larger sized generator and multiple sites could be impacted by a coordinated attack. Attacks could lead to system failures lasting for years and resulting in chronic shortages in resources (food, fuel, communications, etc.).

We can put EMP in perspective with regard to the potential economic and societal costs: the 14 August 2003 blackout, $4-10 billion; Hurricane Katrina, $140-300 billion; severe geomagnetic storm scenario, $1-2 trillion in first year and depending on damage full recovery could take 4-10 years. The EMP costs do not take into account secondary and tertiary impacts. All sorts of electronic devices, not directly impacted by the EMP, could be damaged or rendered useless due to the unavailability of electricity. Widespread failure of the electronic infrastructure will place millions of lives at risk. Major emphasis should be focused on preventing solar storm, EMP, and IEMI related catastrophic failures with remedial design measures to block the effects of GIC and measures to harden the electric and communications infrastructures.

Mr. Ron Plesco, Esq., *CEO – National Cyber Forensics Training Alliance.* Mr. Plesco's presentation focused on cyber security threats as catastrophic infrastructure events. The mission of the National Cyber Forensics Training Alliance (NCFTA) is to identify, mitigate and neutralize cyber threats. The NCFTA is a nonprofit organization that desires to gather the cyber community, share threat information, and (legally) deal with the threats. The NCFTA receives support from international law enforcement and industry in 34 countries.

Mr. Plesco addressed workshop attendees to highlight the depth and magnitude of the cyber threat. The landscape includes organized crime triads which concentrate their effort on institutional accounts and vendor software and hardware. The victims include banks, individual accounts via ATM disabling authentication, and the stock market, where malware can obtain system administrator user names and passwords. Internet switches and routers are stolen by bad actors, modified, and resold to enable the theft of information that flows through them. A class of malware, known as an advanced persistent threat, sits on a network and steals information such as accounts and passwords while running off of botnets. Such botnets are often found in social networks as well as banking and government networks aimed at illicitly stealing credentials and money.

Other areas of cyber theft are found in integrated circuit chips used for point of sale machines such as credit card swipe devices modified for criminal use. Malware can cause generators and other infrastructure to go offline, target telecom services for the misuse of bandwidth, and other malicious activities such as payroll account fund routing, diversion of payroll by creating fake employees, and can disarm home security systems. Crime triads have even leveraged outsourcing to India, where illicit work is performed by unsuspecting companies. In general, the combination of commercial off-the-shelf software and connectivity to the internet open governments, businesses, and critical infrastructure (such as trains, waste water systems, and power plants) to cyber attack.

Mr. Rich Caverly, *Department of Homeland Security National Response Framework.* Mr. Caverly's presentation was entitled "Enhancing Resilience and Protecting the Nation's Critical Infrastructure." He defined critical infrastructure as assets, systems, and networks that are vital to society and devastating if impaired. The federal government can respond to Critical Infrastructure and Key Resources (CIKR) incidents under the provisions of the Robert T. Stafford Disaster Relief and Emergency Assistance Act. The Stafford Act allows the Federal Emergancy Management Agency (FEMA) to assist and coordinate federal agencies, but not direct the entire operation. The federal government does not have the ability or authority to support the private sector to rebuild infrastructure, provide security, move law enforcement across state lines, or any other function that the private sector can provide for itself. Damage to infrastructure may have impacts well beyond immediate disaster area and produce cascading effects.

There are two components to effective federal response – the National Response Framework (NRF) and National Infrastructure Protection Plan. The federal government does not own emergency response and recovery – the States do. The federal government supports the States as necessary. However, the reality is that when the federal government goes in to respond, it usually takes a greater role than constitutionally described. For example, a national contingency plan was used for oil spills. The NRF CIKR support annex describes what support will be provided, how to bring in additional resources, and assistance levels. Everything that the DHS does needs to be fed down to the local level. The federal government doesn't tell how to restore capability, but rather it brings technical assistance and resources to bear on the problem. The Joint Field Office provides a unified coordination group and a unified coordination staff, as well as an infrastructure liaison and CIKR support staff. What should be asked for to help in a critical infrastructure response is based on public safety and health considerations. These issues include the requestor's capability to resource itself, alternative means and timing, benefit to the restoration of a local community CIKR, benefits to meeting national needs, and the potential cost share by requestor. The framework is addressing partnerships at different levels – national/regional/state/local sector – and creation of fusion cells to share information within a specific region/locality. Information sharing is key and there are homeland security information network critical servers at fusion centers and emergency operations centers. Decision makers need to see information to make decisions, while information is being processed in "stovepipes" (energy, water, etc.). The fusion of these stovepipe systems needs to be accomplished somehow. There are some infrastructures that share information better than others. Credentialing access to information is a huge issue for CIKR personnel when passage and access are time critical issues. An emerging notion is the importance of communicating with the private sector in order to relieve local authorities and emergency responders from restoration work by bringing in the Wal-Mart/Home Depot-like supply chain to restore operations. A willingness from private and public sectors to sustain this relationship is growing. (See Q&A at Annex A)

Mr. Rich Haver, *Defense Science Board: Unconventional Operational Concepts and the Homeland.* Mr. Haver opened his segment with Secretary of Defense Rumsfeld's challenge to the Defense Science Board (DSB) on how to fight the next war. The sanctuary of the U.S. homeland had been an assumption in the past. The 2007 DSB Summer Study was entitled "Challenges to Military Operations in Support of U.S. Interests."

While we have been fighting two wars, the adversary has been learning how to decimate the United States. The DSB presumed that an informed and educated enemy wants to bring the world to its knees, and knows U.S. vulnerabilities. There are three imperatives: 1) this is a serious problem that isn't getting the attention it needs; 2) it cannot be solved easily or inexpensively and trade-offs will need to be made; 3) there is an ample body of information beyond unclassified that indicates this is not an unthought-of concept by the enemy. There are many reasonable and unreasonable expectations for homeland defense. The reasonable expectations are the sharing of information and the protection against air, missile, and sea attack. The unreasonable expectations are the protection against or detection and production of weapons of mass destruction in the United States, the protection of civil infrastructure against initial attack, and the constant surveillance of land and maritime borders. There have been very few real efforts to stress the system. The exercises are too light and not realistic. Our nation should train as it intends to fight. With lots of excuses, there is no progress leaving the United States completely unprepared.

Taking Hurricane Katrina as an example, it took a lot of DOD resources to respond on an adequate scale. The only agency capable of global reach, infrastructure, capability, discipline is the DOD, so this scenario will continue. The worse the event, the more likely the DOD will be called upon. But it must be remembered that there are many interdependencies – factories that support each other and the military, the energy needed to run them, and the people who operate them are all mutually dependent. There needs to be a listing of critical infrastructure and their mutual dependencies. There is a need for contingency plans too, for instance paying employees in cash when the banking infrastructure is disrupted or collapsed. Provisions like this need to be included in DOD contracts to ensure these types of contingency plans and actions are in place. Consequence management is the biggest gap in dealing with WMD. There should be incentives for military families to prepare for a catastrophic event. The selling point to the military personnel is that they cannot protect our nation if they cannot protect themselves or their families. This is leadership by example, to build in the capability to have two weeks of provisions and self-sustainment at home. This is a matter of national will and confidence. The enemy is looking for a means to hurt us asymmetrically and we must prepare for that. And we do that with the DOD stating emphatically that this is important and by making a more proactive DOD and DHS partnership.

Mr. Haver closed with a WMD briefing. He considered this a wake-up call for leadership. The armed services are prepared, but no one else seems to be. That is why the EMP commission's reports are seen as good news. At least there was acknowledgement that there is a problem. The enemy is addressing how to employ WMD to get more bang for the buck, where the emotional effect is at the top of all other effects. An informed and educated enemy is assessing its employment. There has been post-Cold War lethargy toward nuclear capability. We need to care again, after 15 years of neglect by senior leadership that has impacted operational knowledge, readiness, expertise, force options, survivability, and support of new critical infrastructure. This needs to be part of the public dialogue which takes national leadership to do, even if there is a political price for it. (See Q&A at Annex A.)

Mr. Robert Farmer, *Federal Emergency Management Agency (FEMA)*. Mr. Farmer's presentation was "Military/Community Planning for a Catastrophic Critical Infrastructure Event." He described DHS/FEMA as a very different organization after Hurricane Katrina. The Post-Katrina Emergency Management Reform Act provided new authorities that enable FEMA to do things such as move personnel and equipment pre-disaster rather than having to wait until a disaster had been declared. FEMA's mission is to work as a member of the team to enable and to support our citizens and first responders to ensure that as a nation we work together to build, sustain, and improve our capability to prepare for, protect against, respond to, recover from, and mitigate the effects of a catastrophe.

FEMA has 10 regions where the work gets done. The biggest mission is Quadrennial Homeland Security Review, Mission 5, to ensure resilience. A measure of success is the extent to which the citizenry is engaged and involved. FEMA is working on communications. The website www.ready.gov can help, but more can be done to help the citizenry prepare for emergencies. A major goal is to use funding to build resiliency in communities by training firefighters, first responders, and emergency managers. FEMA must first ask state and local agencies to participate and there are costs associated, but FEMA hopes to build synergy and partnerships.

FEMA is the steward of The National Response Framework (NRF), which is a re-write of the National Response Plan. The framework establishes key principles, roles, responsibilities, and high level doctrine for disaster response. There is a mechanism in place to bring in and engage other government agencies in the response process. The real work is down at the regional level to ascertain what work can be done. There are multiple jurisdictions when dealing with events: local governments, state and tribal governments, private sector and non-governmental organizations, and the federal government, generating lots of negotiation and little directing. The Incident Command System provides staff structure that reports to the incident commander. FEMA also coordinates with the DOD and has two representatives with USNORTHCOM as well as with other DOD agencies.

There are a number of pre-scripted mission sets now prepared such as mortuary services, aero-medical patient evacuation, and national water assets. Preparation for an emergency really is a whole community effort. The "Whole Community" methodology is built upon a foundation of mega-scenarios consisting of the maximum challenges across a range of scenarios. Such ideas begin to build a framework for catastrophic planning. The New Madrid mega-scenario involves a 7 million person population over 25,000 square miles across 8 states and several FEMA regions. It depicts 190,000 fatalities in the initial hours of the event and 265,000 citizens require emergency medical attention. There is severe damage to critical infrastructure, key resources and essential transportation infrastructure, with limited ingress and egress options. This scenario does not address EMP/EMI, but for starters, this should be enough of a challenge with all normal structures failing. (See Q&A at Annex A)

Mr. Henry Schwartz, *CEO, Founder of Stueben Foods and EMPAct America* (video presentation). This presentation was by video by the not for profit, non government EMPact America to address EMP issues. To view this video and other related resources, go to www.empactamerica.org.

Mr. John Schauffert, *U.S. Northern Command, NCJ34 Assessments Branch Chief.* Mr. Schauffert's presented an overview of USNORTHCOM's Defense Critical Infrastructure (DCIP) Program. The risk calculation is given by the formula Risk = (criticality x vulnerability x threat). Defense critical infrastructure is a composite of DOD and non-DOD assets essential to support and sustain military forces and operations worldwide. Defense Critical Assets (DCAs) are of extraordinary importance such that, if they suffer degradation, the DOD would be incapable of accomplishing its military mission.

The DOD has a critical asset identification process prioritized into three tiers. Tier One assets that are subsequently categorized as defense critical assets are assessed once every three years by the Mission Assurance Division out of Dahlgren, Maryland. They are the assessment execution arm of Assistant to the Secretary of Defense for Homeland Defense and America's Security Affairs, who is the DOD Program Manager for DCAs. Asset owners are ultimately responsible for remediating any deficiencies identified in the assessment. The assistant Secretary of Defense approves remediation efforts for DCAs. Tier 1 Task Critical Assets contain the most important assets, where the loss could have devastating impact on the ability of DOD to accomplish its mission. In 2011 there may be a deeper look into cyber and/or EMP. The DOD is almost completely dependent on the external electrical grid as DOD installation generator power is generally limited in duration. USNORTHCOM's provides the J3 and the commander a report on events and analysis, potential impact to mission, and the impact on critical infrastructure.

USNORTHCOM's Defense Support to Civil Authority (DSCA) mission, which requires visibility on Civil Critical Infrastructure, is built on cooperation, collaboration, and voluntary mutual information sharing. It is a work in progress with the civilian sector. The DOD cannot direct the civilian sector to do anything, so it must depend on relationships and collaboration. The geographic combatant commanders (GCCs) will act to prevent or mitigate the loss or degradation of DOD-owned critical assets within the area of responsibility along with other DOD components. Asset owners have this as a primary responsibility, however since USNORTHCOM does have a force protection mission, it can set conditions and increase security to protect some of these assets.

There are numerous defense infrastructure sector lead agents: the defense industrial base (Defense Contract Management Agency), financial services (Defense Finance and Accounting Service), global information grid (Defense Information Systems Agency), health affairs (Assistant Secretary of Defense for Health Affairs), intelligence (surveillance and recon, Defense Intelligence Agency), logistics (Defense Logistics Agency), and personnel (Defense Human Resource Activity), as examples. DHS is the lead agency for the protection of the national critical infrastructure. The DOD can be called upon to protect National Critical Infrastructure but only when directed by the President. In a DSCA scenario such as Hurricane Katrina, DOD was called in to save lives and protect property. In this instance visibility on availability of civil infrastructure is critical in DSCA operational decision making. DoD was able to gain the necessary visibility of civilian infrastructure by partnering with federal agencies by event and impact reporting and analysis. On a daily basis, USNORTHCOM provides information to DOD on any degradation or significant damage to a defense critical asset, task critical asset, or a defense industrial base critical asset.

Mr. James Platt, *HQDA DAMMO-ODP: Force Protection.* Mr. Platt's presentation was entitled "Integration of Emergency Management of Critical Infrastructure at Department of the Army." The Army is playing catch-up with emergency management but it is establishing many mutual aid agreements needed between installations and local communities. Army installations must tie into critical infrastructure as well, so there is a mission to protect and restore these assets. This is a related but different mission from the Defense Support to Civil Authority (DSCA) mission since the Army provides forces to USNORTHCOM and must protect its bases in order to project needed forces. The Army must be able to deliver combat capability to the GCCs. The Army provides critical infrastructure risk management by identifying redundant or alternate capabilities and presents them to the GCCs to review options. The person completing the assessment may not completely understand the GCCs' needs, timelines, or what other assets are available. The person conducting the assessment must conduct the review using a system of systems approach. This approach has proven difficult and the Army is still working through this process.

Not all vulnerabilities can be mitigated but they can be normalized and prioritized to support the defense global mission. Electrical energy is a critical issue for everyone, and we must find a way to mitigate any degradation to this asset and resolve challenges in the relationships between national and DOD critical infrastructure. This calls for integrating Department of the Army prioritization for infrastructure restoration with local, state and federal agencies. Similarly, the National Incident Management System calls for implementation of mutual aid between the Army and its community partners. There is a plan for "islanding" assets on military installations, but there are surrounding private sector and civilian community issues to resolve. The website http://www.acsim. army.mil/readyarmy/ provides military families with information on how to provide for themselves for a short time. The information is aimed towards deployed soldiers so they can have a degree of confidence that their families are protected and safe while protecting the nation.

Mr. Timothy Sevison, *Deputy Director, Pennsylvania Emergency Management Agency (PEMA)*. Presentation: "Military Planning for a Catastrophic Critical Infrastructure Event." PEMA had its beginnings in 1951 for civil defense and became known as PEMA in 1978. It added counterterrorism planning to its mission in 2002, and by executive order in 2007 it is now part of the Office of Homeland Security. PEMA's emergency response plan details 15 emergency support functions and is responsible for government and emergency management, preparedness, resilience, and catastrophic planning. Each state has an emergency management agency (EMA) of some sort, which can be any combination of military and civilian entities, state police, and other state officials. For emergency management purposes, Pennsylvania is divided into three regions. Geographic regions may be different among the various agencies within the state. For instance, National Guard geographic regions may be different than the state police regions. There are other variations as well. For example, Pennsylvania support functions are similar but not the same as FEMA's. The main point here is to highlight the need to be aware of the variations in each state's EMA organizations and functions. By law, local elected officials in Pennsylvania have command during an incident, and in the state that means there are 2,566 potential local commanders. Sheriffs are not law enforcement officers in Pennsylvania, as in other states, such as Oklahoma and Texas. Other political subdivisions are significant as well, such as school districts and other commissions. Elected officials are responsible for the health, safety, and welfare of the citizens within their jurisdiction, and therefore in Pennslvania, they must appoint an emergency management coordinator for each of the 2,566 municipalities. Each county has an appointed emergency management coordinator but counties are not resource rich and must use local resources. In this state the governor can delegate to his or her emergency management agency for coordination; first responders are almost all volunteers, with the exception of law enforcement; emergency management is almost all volunteer; emergency medicine is about half volunteer; and fire services are about 90 percent volunteer. When an incident arises, PEMA collects information to substantiate a declaration of an emergency for the governor to issue. The emergency management council must meet within 72 hours to ratify the declaration, which can mobilize the National Guard, suspend statutes, and invoke a quarantine, among other things. The state has nine regional task forces based on natural boundaries and each has specific capabilities. Preparedness and resilience are tied to FEMA's www.ready.gov website and are predicated on a Citizen Corps program consisting of volunteers for neighborhood watch, volunteer firemen, and volunteer websites that route individuals to appropriate types of services based on interests and skills. One of the biggest challenges is to instill a 72-hour personal sustainment mindset for individuals and families. Additional challenges are family support for first responders and other emergency management personnel, nuclear power plants, hazard mitigation plans and strategies, DHS/FEMA catastrophic planning initiatives (New Madrid, improvised nuclear device), regional catastrophic planning initiatives (with New York/New Jersey), exit flow from New York and New Jersey, and presidential and gubernatorial initiatives (Project PREPARE, Children in Disaster).

Dr. William Fortschen, *Author, "One Second After"* (via teleconference). Refer to the Q&A Annex at the end of this report.

Dr. Peter Vincent Pry, *EMP Commission, President EMPAct America, Director U.S. Nuclear Strategy Forum.* Presentation on the role of the EMP Commission. Dr. Pry stated that many do not understand the role of congressional commissions in helping law makers forge national security policy. Congressional commissions and presidential commissions serve as instruments of last resort, when the defense and intelligence communities cannot form a consensus on some issue of vital importance to national security, such as "What is the significance of EMP?" A single commission, because of its great expertise and powers, historically has been sufficient to resolve major controversies and establish new directions in national security policy. Ironically, the EMP Commission, despite making a compelling case that the very existence of the United States is threatened by U.S. unpreparedness to cope with nuclear or natural EMP threats, has not been as successful as past commissions in moving the U.S. Government (USG) to defend the American people. Nor has the USG acted to defend civilian infrastructures from EMP despite an EMP threat from Russia to paralyze U.S. civilian critical infrastructures, uttered in the face of a U.S. Congressional delegation during a U.S.-Russian meeting in Vienna in May 1999 attempting to resolve the Balkans crisis, when NATO was bombing Serbia, Russia's historical ally. Nor has the USG acted to defend civilian infrastructures from EMP despite an EMP threat from Russian President Medvedev in 2008, shortly after the election of President Obama, warning that Russia would not tolerate the Bush Administration's NATO missile shield, and that Russia would take steps to neutralize it. Nor has the USG acted to protect its civilian critical infrastructures from EMP despite Commission recommendations to do so, and despite the EMP Commission representing the greatest body of expertise on this threat in the Free World.

The EMP Commission did experiments in simulators to see how vulnerable electronics were to EMP, some experiments that were never before conducted, and proved definitively that modern electronics are over one million times more vulnerable to EMP than the electronics of the 1960s – and are becoming increasingly more vulnerable. The EMP Commission also proved that EMP is not merely a theoretical, physics-based threat. The EMP Commission proved that the threat is real. Iran, North Korea, China and Russia have conducted EMP research and, in open source writings, describe attacking the United States with EMP. Moreover, Iran has conducted several missile tests to detonate at high altitudes, as if practicing EMP attacks. Yet despite all this evidence that EMP is a clear and present danger, while the USG deserves credit for implementing EMP Commission recommendations to protect U.S. military forces, it deserves condemnation for failing to protect U.S. civilian critical infrastructures from EMP. Given our current state of unpreparedness, within 12 months of an EMP attack or a "great" geomagnetic storm, an estimated two-thirds of the U.S. population would perish from starvation and societal collapse.

Why has the USG failed to act on the EMP Commission's recommendations to protect civilian critical infrastructures? Congress has tried to implement the EMP Commission's recommendations. However, our biggest EMP vulnerability is not technological, but bureaucratic and cultural. Congress has so far been unable to make progress protecting the civilian critical infrastructures because it cannot overcome jurisdictional "turf" rivalries between competing congressional committees who veto each other's efforts to protect the infrastructures. DHS so far refuses even to include EMP as a national planning scenario, arguing that defending against a nuclear EMP attack is outside DHS jurisdiction, and is a DOD responsibility. The DOD so far refuses any responsibility for protecting civilian critical infrastructures from EMP because these infrastructures are under the jurisdiction of DHS. Moreover, since a catastrophic EMP could be caused by a great geomagnetic storm, such natural disasters clearly are the responsibility of DHS, according to DOD. So while the bureaucrats continue to argue, no progress is being made protecting the civilian critical infrastructures from EMP. This is an added benefit for the enemy to exploit. Our bureaucratic barriers are a vulnerability for us, not like the enemy whose totalitarian and authoritarian systems do not allow such democratic foibles as legal jurisdiction to get in their way. (See Q&A at Annex A.)

Colonel Doug Schueler, *Deputy Commander, Joint Task Force-Civil Support (JTF-CS)*. Presentation: "JTF-CS 101 Briefing." The JTF-CS was established in 1999 to better respond to chemical, biological, radiological, nuclear and high yield explosive (CBRNE) incidents. It was originally established under the Joint Forces Command, but is now aligned under U.S. Army North (ARNORTH), which is the Army Component Commander/Joint Forces Land Component Commander (JFLCC) for USNORTHCOM. JTF-CS is organized to plan, anticipate and respond to catastrophic CBRNE incidents. There is a CBRNE focus during steady state operations and also for planning, preparing, and supporting national exercises and special events (for example, UN General Assembly sessions). It acts in support of the local jurisdiction and leadership. Its consequence management capabilities range from the most likely (high yield explosives) to the most catastrophic (nuclear weapons). JTF-CS is organized with specialized task forces for operations, aviation and medical. The incident analysis cell does the anticipation work and the 'what if' review and analysis. The joint planning augmentation cell (JPAC) has exportable planning expertise. The emergency plans analysis team does analysis to gain understanding of the capabilities and limitations at the local and state level. JTF-CS utilizes interagency liaison officers to enhance unity of effort. (See Q&A at Annex A.)

SECTION 3: Workshop Group Break-out Sessions

Group A: Theme – Preparation (Professor Bernie Griffard, Moderator)

Group A was responsible for brainstorming the preparation for an EMP event in the United States and making recommendations for next step actions to better prepare for such a situation. Its central question was: "How does the United States prepare for an EMP attack?" It recognized that any good plan must plan for the worst case scenario and it addressed both solar and nuclear weapon EMP events. Solar storms, the group argued, had broader global impact than a hostile weapon initiated EMP attack, whereas a weapons-based EMP event had more depth and would be more catastrophic on a local and national scale.

Either class of EMP initiation requires pre-incident planning and preparation. Although pre-event course of action (COA) development might be left primarily to the DOD, the group strongly urged the whole of U.S. government and all of society to get involved with planning and preparation. The group advocated that the DHS should orchestrate a "National Back-up Power Day" to test down to the household level the state of preparation in the event that commercial grid electrical power is lost on a regional or national scale. Such a practice day would initially highlight the vulnerabilities, weaknesses, dependencies, and immediacy for back-up power sources. The group further argued that EMP must be integrated into the National Security Framework in a layered approach which would address the power grid, communications, water and sanitation, food, and all levels of societal necessities.

The group emphatically recommended that the "Grid Act" (H.R. 5026, Grid Reliability and Infrastructure Defense [GRID] Act), which passed in the House of Representatives on Jun 9, 2010, needs to be passed by the U.S. Senate. Passage would also include one hundred military facilities to be "power independent" so that they could survive as a launch point for support recovery operations in the event of power grid failure. On a smaller and more immediate scale, the group proposed that EMP be included in the

Joint Forces Command exercise "Unified Quest" and the Joint Capability Technology Demonstration called SPIDERS (Smart Power Infrastructure Demonstration for Energy Reliability and Security) in FY11, as outlined by USPACOM and USNORTHCOM (found at: http://hawaii.gov/dbedt/info/ energy/efficiency/RebuildHawaiiConsortium/Events/PastEvents/2010-03-10/ SPIDERS%20for%20D.C.%20-%20Feb%202010.pdf). In its summary, the group recommended the development of an EMP national planning scenario and the development of acquisition strategy to begin planning and preparation for an EMP attack.

Group B: Theme – Initial Response (Mr. William Waddell, Moderator)

Group B predicated its discussion on three imperatives for an initial response to an EMP attack. There would be infrastructure failure, local authorities would be overwhelmed, and military capabilities would be degraded. The group postulated that initial response to a critical infrastructure failure depends heavily on pre- event preparation. DSCA would assist civil recovery operations, but (as the group concluded) only to the extent of what capabilities remain after assuring national sovereignty. This observation in fact reflects the "spectrum of recovery" conclusions independently arrived at by Group C, discussed in the next part.

Group B set forth a number of tasks which were deemed essential to properly respond to initial post-attack conditions as follows:

1. Seek support via DSCA
2. Rely on pre-established mission sets
3. Provide assets when requested
4. Assess damage
5. Establish direct communications with the State and National Guard headquarters

The group recommended that the DOD establish communications at all levels, assist with the restoration of utilities (water, sanitation, power) and with logistical support. In addition, the group recommended that a variety of scenarios should be reviewed for DSCA support activities in an EMP environment. It also encouraged the support of recommendations of the EMP Commission. Group B's overarching observation was that initial response relies heavily on electric power and that its protection and restoration is essential. The nation would be best served by preparing now with EMP hardening of critical infrastructures before an event and that the most critical of these infrastructures are communications and the generation and distribution of electric power.

Group C: Theme – Recovery (Mr. Jeff Caton, Moderator)

Group C was charged with determining post-EMP event recovery potentials. After setting forth basic fundamentals and assumptions which included the fact that electricity is the key enabling infrastructure, a "spectrum of recovery" diagram was put forth with regard to DOD reactions and priorities. Whereas the U.S. military will support the restoration of infrastructure and civil order, the diagram depicted how the DSCA mission area, primarily codified in DOD Directive 5111.13, would become less involved in such restoration as the DOD's primary mission areas increased, thus shifting the civil support burden to Homeland Defense. In other words, as the conditions become direr, the DOD will be more concerned with U.S. sovereignty than civil assistance.

The group determined that the foundation to all recovery is centered on the individual and the group called for a civil defense renaissance likened to the 1950's nuclear attack preparedness. The group set forth several implications as a result: first, that the number one job of the DOD will be to reestablish and protect core warfighting capabilities; second, that strategic communications is the key enabler for post-EMP recovery; and lastly, that application of Cold War planning methodologies is advised, which include pre-planned/pre-formatted messages and well-established and exercised "devolution of command." Deployed U.S. military forces outside of the continental United States are to be considered a strategic asset during the recovery phase of an EMP attack. The group set forth a number of recommendations:

1. Develop discrete EMP event planning scenarios as follows:

    a. Worst Case: Continental EMP event threat to sovereign rule that is irreversible to previous normal conditions (lowest probability)

    b. Middle Case: Regional EMP threat to support systems

    c. Solar Case: Primarily a threat to electrical infrastructure that is largely reversible and recoverable, but may require time (highest probability)

2. Establish an Integrated National Recovery Priority Plan for an EMP event and exercise it regularly:

    a. Implement Congressional EMP Commission Report (2004 & 2008) recommendations as appropriate

    b. All Agencies must address requirements for extended recovery from long-duration event (i.e., years long)

    c. Combatant Commands have integrated OPLANs for worst case scenario in place to include potential use of OCONUS forces as a strategic reserve

3. All U.S. Agencies should develop and exercise contingency plans for likely EMP events to include re-examining the concept of strategic reserves of critical materials and technical skills required for recovery.

4. Move from a "preparedness" to a "resiliency" doctrine (i.e., planning beyond the "preparedness" timeframe which only accounts for a 72 hour response)

5. Develop integrated partnerships with Industry to provide incentives to harden future systems to EMP effects:

    a. Emphasize systems that would be assets to recovery

    b. Ensure key employees are available during recovery

    c. Determine requirements for EMP hardened C3+ Systems (DOD/USG/State/Local Gov/Critical Industries)

SECTION 4: Workshop Conclusions and Recommendations

The "In the Dark" workshop provided an invaluable forum to bring together a wide-range of perspectives on national catastrophic infrastructure failure. The plenary session provided attendees informative and updated information on the threats to infrastructure, the source of threats, government agency preparation activities, and planning scenarios. It also provided analysis from individuals in the private sector, as well as an EMP Commission expert and a topical book author. This session served to ground the attendees in the ends, ways, and means of dealing with infrastructure failure, and just as importantly, with the current state of preparation in the event of such an event. More specifically, the plenary session highlighted the two most critical infrastructures – electricity and communications – and the two most likely causes for their possible failure – geomagnetic induced currents due to a solar storm and electromagnetic pulse (EMP) most likely occurring from a high altitude nuclear explosion. The attendees (see Annex B) represented all levels of government from mayor, county commissioner, state emergency management, federal Department of Energy, and private industry to name only a few. Consequently, question and answer periods during the plenary session represented a broad cross-section of views, concerns, and constituencies which ensured that a full-range of problem sets was being addressed.

Armed with current information, the break-out groups honed in on three specific areas of interest and concern: the preparation for the loss of electric and communications on a massive scale; the initial response to the loss of these two critical infrastructures; and the probable unfolding of events during the period of recovery. Whereas the specific conclusions of the break-out sessions were delineated in the previous section, there are some generalities that can be stated with regard to all three break-out groups:

1. There is very little in the way of back-up capability to the electric grid (upon which the communications infrastructure is vitally dependent). Individual homes rarely have an independent source of electric power, industry has some continuity of operations (COOP) capability, and essential services such as hospitals are required to have a few days of auxiliary power to sustain them off of the power grid. The likely scenarios caused by solar storms and EMP forecast a power grid loss for many times longer than current backup power sources, maybe even a year or more if a significant number of high power transformers are destroyed and would have to be re-manufactured. In some cases, such grid components are manufactured off-shore causing even more delay. The net effect of the collapse of the electric grid is that communities would become localized and insular. They would be disconnected from the more regional conditions, the possibility of outside assistance such as food and medicine, and the chances of recovery to normal. One group even explored that there might be no return to normal as was previously known.

2. There is little in the way of preparation for the loss of the electric grid. Although there actually is a significant amount of information in the form of literature, websites, and planning from the local government to the federal agency level, there has been little effort in the form of individual preparation and rehearsal for such an event. This includes the stockpiling of food and survival kits to include radios in Faraday protection boxes with batteries and first aid supplies. Preparing for months without a commercial source of clean water (city water pressure is often dependent on electric pumping to storage towers) and stoppage of sewage treatment facilities will require new methods of survival particularly in populated areas. This

overarching condition permeated all break-out groups which called for better communication to individual households, education, and even practice days without electricity on a variety of scales. In a clear sense, this workshop highlighted the interconnectedness of the three breakout groups as a triad of interdependencies where initial response to grid loss is dependent on preparation and recovery is dependent on both. The root of all post-event activities is the adequacy of addressing the problem in advance. The passage of H.R. 5026 would initiate the demonstration of one hundred "grid independent" military installations, but it appears that it would be a considerably longer time before a modicum of independence and training would reach all corners of the nation.

3. Department of Defense response to electric grid infrastructure failure would be measured and exercised based on the level of the threat to the sovereignty of the nation. It is always the case that local governments (technically) are in charge during a crisis and the DOD is always in support of civilian authority. Whereas the DOD will provide support and assistance in the restoration of infrastructure failures to the greatest extent possible, it too has limitations in personnel and funding, and the possibility of regional and national grid failure could push the DOD beyond its ability to assist on a massive scale. What is clear, as emphasized by each break-out group, is that the national defense responsibilities of the DOD will come first when there is a question of allocating resources.

These generalized conclusions from the three break-out groups should be considered in context with the recommendations from each group. Noted here, as well as during the plenary session discussions, there is clearly a need for the production of more scenarios such as the New Madrid mega-scenario developed by FEMA. Just as medical facilities conduct mass casualty exercises, realistic scenarios at a variety of levels need to be developed by local, state, and regional levels and then exercised. No one doubts the difficulty in doing this, but the consequences of not being prepared for a catastrophic infrastructure failure would certainly be more disruptive and truly impair life and limb.

In the same manner, the workshop recommended that there be better planning for power grid and communications failures. First responders and emergency management agencies will be the first to be called upon. All problems will appear to be local, even though the failure conditions will be wide-spread.

Better planning and preparation at the local level is the key to initial response to a crisis and the best path to recovery. Indications are that citizens are not as keenly aware of the threat as the nation had been in the 1950's during Cold War civil defense.

Lastly, the workshop recommended better individual preparedness. Survivability is a personal responsibility. The greater the extent of individual preparation the lighter the burden will be on first responders and government to include the DOD. It is the responsibility of the DOD to preserve the nation and maintain a decisive edge to defeat an enemy. In this regard, individual ability to defend one's self contributes to our survival as a nation.

ANNEX A – Selected Question and Answer Sessions

Mr. Pappas Q&A:

Q: Can you put a name to our biggest threats? **A:** Capabilities of Russia, China both trying to be developed (particular to cyber), correlated with their military sales programs. Look at information that can be easily obtained and what scientists are exchanging. These are the types of things we need to take into consideration. TRADOC looks very seriously at what is going on with countries and non-state actors and what harm can be done.

Q: Does DOD differentiate between catastrophic or other, such as genocidal? **A:** Scope of threat. There are countries that want to attack and others that want to annihilate. Existential threat listing is rather limited right now. Cyber for instance, and is being considered. What is a sovereignty ending event?

Q: Pattern implies development of local capability to be resilient; do you agree with this or am I overreaching? **A:** Fair statement. Building capability to manage consequences needs to be done. We are developing leaders to operating in confusing situations. Limited resources that local governments have is a significant issue. Directly to point, we need interaction at all levels to discuss and communicate/exchange information, to understand who can do what and respond as a team.

Q: An article recently published was "military protects military," but does Homeland Security protect everyone and everything else? Cybersecurity is an example. **A:** Yes. Discussions, workshops, exercises have been taking place, but more work is necessary. There are issues with access. Cybersecurity is too complex to find quick answers, so priority will go to priority nets. Not a good answer to the question or problem. **Discussion** among attendees: Two categories: Who and how. The how will help us harden our defenses. Need to ask WHO and HOW, scale of attack/response, and consequences. Will attack be debilitating? What will require military response to prevent and deter. What will be required to be resilient? Interdependencies are critical to understand (between for instance military and need for electricity). Among agencies we need sharing of information and cooperation. Continuity of operations during a crisis is essential as well.

Mr. Caverly Q&A

Q: This seems to be based on an incident. Is there a plan to address a national event? **A:** No national plan but existing plans and partnerships are being discussed and enhanced. Since infrastructure is not centrally controlled and there is no one point for failure, these pockets can be restored as plans allow.

Q: Is there a plan to develop a national plan? **A:** There some efforts to move toward a national plan to address some aspects of the infrastructure, such as electric, but not all.

Q: Are there any plans for addressing personal preparedness or corporate preparedness? **A:** I haven't seen a workable plan yet. Perception of risk needs to change before any plans can be implemented. Risk of terrorist attack was the same on 12 September as it was on 11 September, but the public perception was higher and different. This is key. **Comments:** If local communities can sponsor individual preparedness kits, compliance is better. There are local training programs like the Community Emergency Response Team (CERT), which is not highly publicized, that allows local fire and rescue staff to train individuals to protect themselves and their homes. Again, perception of citizens to see this as important is required. Locales near the gulf take hurricanes more seriously now, for instance.

Q: What kind of monetary process is in placed/planned if the banking system fails? **A:** We are working very closely with the banking system to ensure bases are covered. It may very well be that organizations (Red Cross, Walmart) will be provided those resources to provide for the local community. This is more effective and efficient than the government trying to provide food, bedding and lumber, or logistical stuff, unless there is no system or organizations in place to do so.

Q: Memory fails. Will DHS codify what they do and show improvements to the process? **A:** Yes, we just haven't done it fully yet. What has been documented hasn't been tested. We need to do better, like the military does it (since decision makers and actors change over so frequently). Civilian staff tend to hold onto positions so much longer, so less tendency to document.

Q: How do DHS and FEMA know they can do their job? **A:** Whatever they do depends on the availability of external resources. That is the test.

Q: Generating perception, bringing more players to the table, what can we do (public policy, etc) to ensure we create a sense of opportunity rather than despair? **A:** Leadership. Some are looking at what is needed to be put in place to have a resilient community. FEMA through grant programs can help. It is very good at putting together an ad hoc group, but it is important to bring critical mass to the table and not take all the time trying to figure out if all the right players are there. **Comments:** Those at this table are in a position to speak up and educate. We took this out of the schools. We have fire drills; why not include more in local education efforts? When are we going to tell people how to take care of themselves in the event of a catastrophic event? It has to be now, not at the time of the event. Everyone here has the capability to push this effort forward by preparing locals and pushing policy from government. Lots of great FEMA manuals are out there and available, but the average citizen is unaware and here government leadership has failed. All communities are competing for the same funding, which is problematic. Federal government identifies key CIKR and if not at the top of the order, then there is a long wait.

Q: Are you aware of exercises or planning efforts that envision a time then DHS and DOD change roles for a large scale issue? **A:** For a catastrophic event, probably not. What is the threshold event or events that would allow DOD to be in charge? What is the issue? Then there is the issue of the National Guard and that status. One of the primary resources as a federal responder should be deferring to the local governor, generally. **Comment:** There is not known to be a single scenario where the DOD would take charge, and perhaps there will be many, many players involved. At the end of the day, locals are in charge, even in a multiple state event. But a good precedent would be the Coast Guard (under DHS) and its involvement. It would probably take a state saying it cannot constitutionally remain a state. Until that time, it is very situational. It is know who is in charge, but responders often don't practice it. And communication isn't practiced either.

Mr. Haver Q&A

Q: From a local government perspective, can we practice martial law to protect infrastructure/communication capabilities? How far can we go? **A:** It is the federal government's responsibility to think strategically and communicate. What does it take to make the price unacceptable? The locals can think and act tactically, but not strategically. Pre-Cold War, time was on our side; post-Cold War jihadist era, time is no longer on our side. We have to plan and take decisive action. Make sure the enemy knows his goals are unattainable, and then have the will to flex power.

Q: How do we keep DOD from defending everything? **A:** By working in partnership with DHS to understand roles, responsibilities, vulnerabilities, capabilities, etc. Work with intelligence community to penetrate the penetrators to get into the enemy's mind. This will help to prioritize what we can protect and harden. By providing information to DHS, they can ensure execution of plans.

Mr. Farmer Q&A

Q: Does FEMA stockpile food around the nation? **A:** No. It used to, but no longer. Competition with local business and shelf life were two major issues. FEMA's model is now to serve as the National Logistics Coordinator ensures the flow of required supplies. FEMA does stockpile some items based on our experience. Goal is to be good stewards of the taxpayer dollars for use for specific events.

Q: What about food that is not available (grain reserves gone) or when the entire food network is down? **A:** We are using exercises to sort out what we don't know. We haven't specifically confronted this issue.

Q: What about U.S. Department of Agriculture stockpiles? **A:** There are small caches of items for very immediate needs, first responder needs (maybe first 72 hours?). But there are no catastrophic stockpiles. We received some support from other countries via the State Department for Hurricane Katrina. FEMA works with private sector extensively to ascertain their capabilities and shelf life of available food. There are resources, and FEMA needs to leverage what is available. For instance, FEMA has told planning teams to plan for 72 hours, after that FEMA has national capabilities to leverage resources.

Q: How do you reconcile events that occur over regional lines? **A:** Hurricane Katrina is a prime example. There is a unified coordination group that will adjudicate and prioritize those issues that cross regional lines, and if necessary, it can be adjudicated at the national level.

Q: There was an exercise in Colorado earlier this year. Do you have any comments regarding this exercise that related to the grid? **A:** This was not a FEMA exercise, but there was some FEMA participation.

Q: Is there a clearing house for the results of the various exercises? **A:** Yes, the National Exercise Program (NEP) on the FEMA site (see http://www.fema.gov/prepared/exercise.shtm)

Dr. William Fortschen, author of *One Second After,* by videoconference, Q & A

Q: I would like to challenge the assertion that there is no constituency for EMP preparedness; what is your perspective on the preparedness activists movement? **A:** There are many people working this issue; my call is to make this a political issue, HR 5026, and look what happened to it when it got to Senate. Only when representatives receive 50 or 60 calls do they really look at an issue. So we need to take a more active approach and raise hell with our representatives; maybe then we'll see an impact.

Q: The world is a dangerous place full of potential threats. Limited funding means we cannot manage them all, and practically speaking we end up not defending any. Targeting EMP is important and a critical vulnerably, but each dollar spent on this is a dollar not spend on providing port security which is more vulnerable to rogues. How do we counter this to ensure that it is understood that EMP is a threat as well? (question taken from STRATFOR publication article) **A:** We can look at this like buying a car and taking out the protective measures like air bags. We need to get people to understand that EMP is important, like port security. **Dr. Pry comment:** The STRATFOR article was replete with errors and views of the author only, not even STRATFOR. It fails to include any information as to why the EMP Commission felt that EMP protection was important, and the threats from nations such as Iran and China. Not theoretical threats, but real. I wrote a rebuttal, but STRATFOR did not publish it, but I think STRATFOR removed the original article from its website. (Some of these issues were later addressed in Dr. Pry's presentation) **Discussion**: Concern is that legislators are passing this [STRATFOR] article around. The failure to use the EMP Commission report is inexcusable, as it is a good news story that the commission reported we could be prepared. There is concern that this article is what our lawmakers are taking as legitimate and other private groups as well.

Q: There are sustained efforts by federal agencies working with locals to use exercises to motivate local communities to participate and become resilient. How do we make the sales pitch for a persistent activity that would be effective? **A:** During exercises last year, the most important observation was that culturally we are top down in our decision-making process. In discussion with his local police chief, one person responded that he would immediately contact the county authorities. We have to get everyone to think locally and take action. Think about a world where we have to make all our decisions locally; in an EMP event, this is what we'd have to do, make decisions to deal with the home and community. So we need to have them think through how they (a police chief, for instance) make decisions for our community and what can we do now, such as stockpile transponders to bring communications back up.

Q: Perhaps we can begin looking at the generational piece by having a day without texting, etc., so they can bring this idea home. Is there an educational piece out there?

A: Anyone over 50 can remember civil defense drills. Schools provide excellent opportunity, but we have to get the political will first. We might also get people to think this is an environmental issue, not just a defense issue.

Q: Can you share some medical stories that inspired the book [*One Second After*]? **A:** Newt Gingrich provided a real life story. Shortly after meeting with Newt, a man told him of his father who was in the final weeks of his life, going out like a great cavalry fighter. A storm blew out the electricity at his nursing home and cut this infrastructure. A nurse called and he went to help out, watching his father on a respirator with power provided by a back-up generator. This man asked the attending nurse what would happen if there was no generator backup for electric power. The nurse replied that she'd have to go back to the manual way of respiration, a squeeze ball. She would provide air as long as she could, but would finally get exhausted and the patient would expire. Go to a nursing home and find out how many of patients would die in the first day without the electrical infrastructure. As a culture we need to be aware of this.

Q: T. Boone Pickens, and his recommendations on remaking the grid, your thoughts? **A:** Coalition building makes sense. How much longer would it to do so? We need to build the new 21st century grid that won't be impacted by EMP, safer for America, rather than calling it a smart grid.

Q: Lack of money. Have you run into anything novel that would help how some communities might be handling this? **A:** Not heard of anything particularly novel, mostly common sense. Local municipalities could just go out and spend a few hundred dollars on some walkie-talkies which could provide the basis of a communication system. Citizens can buy a few extra things at the grocery store such as canned goods and rice to provision. This is purchasing fundamental insurance policies without spending a ton of money.

Dr. Pry Q&A

Q: Why not a 16th national planning scenario [isolated EMP event]? **A:** Absolutely, EMP should be included among the DHS national planning scenarios. The EMP Commission worked for 8 years establishing the reality of the EMP threat and devising affordable solutions. There is no excuse for not implementing the EMP Commission recommendations that would take the threat off the table since cost-effective solutions were provided. These solutions would also protect the United States from space storms, cyber threats, sabotage, and natural disasters. The EMP Commission followed an "all hazards" strategy that would protect not just against EMP, but against all potentially catastrophic threats to the infrastructures.

Q: Why isn't this threat sitting on the table of the National Security Council (NSC) to resolve? Why do they risk this catastrophic threat; why ignore since it isn't too expensive to implement? **A:** Good question. No one knows why. It defies good sense. No one really understands. One theory is that in our strategic culture, we prepare for the last crisis. So we are preparing for terrorists like those who hit us on 9/11, like a Pearl Harbor. Even though our enemies are on the verge of obtaining and using this [EMP] threat, unless it happens to someone else, we think it won't happen. That is part of the reason. Another thing about our strategic culture is that, like after 9/11, we are masters of hindsight. Many in the intelligence community claim they anticipated 9/11, because they can point to a paragraph or a sentence in some obscure report. Typically, the intelligence community may anticipate a threat, but not give it enough weight so we will be motivated to do something about it. So, after EMP, someone will pull out an obscure report and falsely claim we were warned, as they did in the aftermath of 9/11. Congress is trying, right now, to protect the country from EMP by passing the Grid Reliability and Infrastructure Defense (GRID) Act (HR 5026) and other legislation. It is very close and the bill might fail. At the presidential level, the Obama Administration (according to press reports) has issued a presidential directive to protect White House Communications from EMP. But this does nothing to protect the average American, and there has been little else. Everyone needs to be educated on the EMP threat. Before the 2004 report was released to the public, no one discussed it and any information and work on it was deeply classified. Despite the release of all this information, there are very few EMP experts, so we need education. The fact that so much about the EMP threat was classified for so long, and that there are so few EMP experts, probably partially accounts for why there has been so little progress. When the EMP Commission report was first released in July 2004, it was on the same day and hour as the release of the 9/11 Commission report, so no one paid attention! The Armed Services Committee takes this seriously, but they don't have jurisdiction over critical civilian infrastructures. The Energy and Commerce Committee has jurisdiction over civilian infrastructures, but few on that Committee have any understanding of the EMP threat. This is the problem. **Discussion**: The electric sector needs to take responsibility for this, but the resolution may not be handled by those who understand it. We need a practical solution that will allow us to resolve the problem. We need action, a new dawning, like when the military finally figured out that they are completely dependent on it. So, we've figured it out, but we have no money. We need electric folks to help solve this. **Dr. Pry comment:** They (NSC) should be a fan of HR 5026 because the federal requirement levels the playing field so all can engage to protect the grid. HR 5026 does provide financial mechanisms to fund EMP protection. HR 5026 also allows the Secretary of Defense to identify 100 bases where electricity will be assured. HR 5026 recognizes that industry must be a vital part of the solution and a leader, and the federal government must work in partnership with industry.

Q: If there is one person in the administration that could take the lead in getting HR 5026 passed, who would it be? **A:** Beyond or in addition to HR 5026, a presidential directive/executive order can do it. The president, with a pen stroke, could protect our nation by directing all relevant departments and agencies to read the EMP Commission report and implement its recommendations. Subsequent research and independent studies have validated the EMP Commission's report and recommendations. DHS has not included the EMP scenario as a baseline for national planning, despite the EMP Commission recommendations and recommendations of several subsequent reports.

Q: What funding is available, what should we buy first (low cost)? **A:** There are several hundred high-energy transformers that are absolutely indispensable to the survival and recovery of the national electric grid that could be protected for as little as $200 million. This minimum investment would at least create the possibility that we could save two-thirds of the American people. It would not guarantee survival and recovery, but would make it possible. Much more can and should be done. If we implemented most of the EMP Commission recommendations, we could neutralize this threat. But we should at least do the bare minimum, and protect those several hundred transformers, or there would be no hope for societal survival and recovery. **Discussion**: There is the Energy Grid Coordination Group in DHS, mandated by Congress, to the DOD's dependence on the grid and reduce the vulnerability to EMP.

COL Schueler Q&A

Q: Does CBRNE include EMP as high explosive or nuclear event? **A:** Right now, there is not a dedicated training scenario for EMP. **Discussion:** Should be included in a nuclear detonation scenario. We know that in a nuclear detonation, there are some EMP effects and plan for that, but not as a single event. **Major Peeke:** Planning is taking place, mostly relating to the level of blast (air, ground). This is why we should probably have the 16th national planning scenario, to plan for the isolated EMP event. **Comment**: Some plans to eliminate the categorization of the (now) 15 planning scenarios; limits planning and outside thinking and locks in people. We are down to 8 now, as we've already gotten rid of a few.

Q: With an EMP attack, how can you implement your plans without resources (delivery systems, for instance)? What kinds of systems do you foresee having and how would you protect them? **A:** As previously briefed, USNORTHCOM has very few assigned forces. From other sources (i.e. JFCOM), we have allocated base response forces. For additional forces, we would submit a request for forces which could be assigned based on availability of forces at the time. The DOD will come into support where other resources may not available or restricted. The National Guard would likely be retained by individual states and are not included in this allocation. So for instance, security will probably be augmented by the National Guard.

Q: What is the opinion of a dual-status, joint forces commander in the state? **A:** We are wrestling with that due to crossing boundaries, federal forces to a state for instance. But it does build in efficiencies.

ANNEX B – Workshop Attendees

NAME	ORGANIZATION
Rick Adrian	Native American Wind Company
George Anderson	Emprimus, LLC
Professor Cynthia Ayers	U.S. Army War College
George Baker	James Madison University
Jena Baker McNeill	The Heritage Foundation
David Bellavia	Vets for Freedom and EMPact America
Rick Blair	Maryland Fire Chiefs, Statewide Alert Network
Harold Brilliant	Mid-Hudson Chiefs of Police Association
Scott Burns	Palo Verde Nuclear Power Plant
Tony Caruana	Supervisor, Town of Tonawanda, New York
Jeff Caton	U.S. Army War College
Jim Caverly	Department of Homeland Security
Colonel Mike Chesney	U.S. Army War College
Ken Chrosniak	U.S. Army War College
Barb Cross	Commissioner, Cumberland County, Pennsylvania
Michael Del Rosso	AcuityTSI
Colonel John Domenech	HQDA Protection Division
Ed Doray	NORAD/USNORTHCOM Interagency Coordination
Robert Farmer	500 C Street WS, Room 820
LTC Gerald Faunce	HQDA G3/5/7 Protector Division
Alan Fleckner MD	Civil Air Patrol
Dottie Fleckner	HAM Radio
Scott Forster	U.S. Army War College
Robin Frazier	Instant Access Networks, LLC
Roger Fraumann	Business Development, Fraumann Associates
Glen Gese	USNORTHCOM J58

NAME	ORGANIZATION
Bernie Griffard	U.S. Army War College
Rich Haver	Northrop Grumman Corporation
Rick Hemphill	Maryland Fire Chiefs, Statewide Alert Network
John Houston	CenterPoint Energy
Ross Howarth	EMPact America
Christopher Huber	U.S. Army North, Provost Marshall Office
Brad Jones	Department of Energy, NNSA/OST
John Kappenman	Storm Analysis Consultants
Bob Kaufmann	EMPact AMERICA
Mick Kicklighter, LTG USA (R)	George Mason University School of Law
Brent Killinger	Dickinson College Police
John LaFond	John LaFond Consulting & KARE-TV
Steve Latshaw	Carlisle Police Department
Wendy LeBlanc	U.S. Army War College
John Lund	U.S. Army, RRMC
Chuck Manto	Instant Access Networks, LLC
Sam Manto	Chicago Police Department
Colonel James Markley	U.S. Army War College
Dillon Martinson	George Mason University School of Law
John A McCarthy	HQDA G3/5/7 Protection Division
Skip Menzies	Maryland Fire Chiefs, Statewide Alert Network
Jason T. Miller	Maryland Fire Chiefs, Statewide Alert Network
David A. Moran	EMPact AMERICA
Steve Mott	Palo Verde Nuclear Power Plant/Engineer
Clifford Mullen	USNORTHCOM
Tom Murray	Carlisle Fire Chief
Brian Nolan	EMPact America
Roland Oliveira	Transtector Systems Inc.
Bob Oreskovic	U.S. Army War College

NAME	ORGANIZATION
Thomas Pappas	TRADOC G2
Scot Peeke	Joint Task Force Civil Support
Sam Pressin	Preparedness
Jim Platt	HQDA G3/5/7 Protection Division (DAMO-ODP)
Ron Plesco Esq.	CEO, National Cyber Forensics Training Alliance
Tom Popik	Geosegment Systems Corporation
Dr. Peter Vincent Pry	Director, Nuclear Strategy Forum
Chris Ramnes	Agent Ops Eastern Command, OST/NNSA
Bill Reeder	EMPact AMERICA
Matt Ryan	The Hershey Company
John Schauffert	USNORTHCOM
Colonel Doug Schueler	Joint Task Force Civil Support
Tim Sevison	Pennsylvania Emergency Management Agency
James Shufelt	U.S. Army War College
Don Spoon	CPGC
AJ Stambaugh	U.S. Army War College
Al Tokar	EMPact America/Steuben Foods
Colonel Bobby Towery	U.S. Army War College
Carl Veach	Pennsylvania State Police
Tom Vinette	U.S. Army War College
William Waddell	U.S. Army War College
Kirk Wilson	Mayor, Carlisle, Pennsylvania
J. Theodore Wise	Department of Public Safety, Cumberland County, Pennsylvania
Paul Wolfe	Defense Intelligence Agency
Chris Yaroch	Department of Energy, NNSA/OST

www.ingramcontent.com/pod-product-compliance
Lightning Source LLC
Chambersburg PA
CBHW070239290526
45789CB00004B/1685